Salad is the English name and first appe:
century with the spelling salad or salad. In addition, th.
origin of the name salad can be varied from the French
spelling salade, Ancient Latin herba Salata and Latin salata.
Salad has been around for a long time, in many different
forms of processing. For example, the Romans, the ancient
Greeks, and the Persians mixed mixed vegetables with a
sauce to eat. Such salads became popular in Europe after the
invasions of the Roman and Greek empires.

Most of the ingredients to make a salad are mainly vegetables with sauces, and depending on the purpose of use, new foods with high protein content such as meat, eggs, etc. or sweet sauces such as ice cream are used to make salads. instead of the familiar vinegar sauce.

The main ingredients of the salad, including:

- Vegetables: Green vegetables (kale, spinach, lettuce, ...), root vegetables (such as cucumbers, tomatoes, bell peppers, ...).
- Fruit: kiwi, apple, avocado,,....
- Fish
- Egg
- Cereal

Coming to this book, you will find recipes for very simple but equally delicious salads for the whole family and friends to enjoy.

What are you waiting for, let's go to the kitchen right away!

Contents

Crab Vegetable Salad

Element

- Vegetable Crab 400 Gr
- Onion 1/4 Bulb
- Cherry tomatoes 200 Gr
- 3 Duck Eggs
- Fish sauce 2 Tbsp

- White Sugar 2 Tablespoons
- Olive Oil 2 Tbsp
- Lemon juice 4 Tbsp
- Chili 2 Fruits
- Garlic 3 Tbsp

Implementation Guide

1. Washed crab claws and soaked them in dilute salt water for about 10 minutes. Then put the vegetables in the refrigerator, let them cool and crisp.

2. Onions are thinly sliced, soaked with vinegar and sugar in the ratio 1:1:2 (1 vinegar: 1 sugar: 2 water) and then put in the refrigerator to keep the onion crisp.

3. Hard-boiled eggs with little salt, peeled and sliced thin. Cherry tomatoes cut in half.

4. Mix the sauce mixture including: 2 tablespoons fish sauce, 2 tablespoons sugar, 2 tablespoons olive oil, 4 tablespoons lemon juice and stir well. Next, add the crushed chili and garlic and mix well.

5. When preparing to eat, mix the crabs, onions, tomatoes and pour the sauce into the mix.

6. Put the mixed vegetables on a plate at this time, put the eggs in so the eggs will not be broken.

Japanese Tofu Salad

Element

- Tomato 1 Fruit
- Young Tofu 1 Piece
- Cabbage 100 Gr
- Sesame Oil 2 Tbsp
- Seasoning Seeds 3 Tablespoons

- Implementation Guide

1. Wash the lettuce and separate them to the right size. Cut tomatoes into slices.

2.Cut the tofu into dices. Put all the spices including: 2 tablespoons sesame oil, 3 tablespoons seasoning seeds, roasted sesame in a small bowl, mix well. Spread the lettuce and tomatoes evenly on a large plate, then spread the tofu on top.

3.Put the tuna and seaweed in turn on top. Drizzle all seasoning on top. So the dish is done

Avocado Chicken Breast Salad

Element

- Avocado 1 Fruit
- Lettuce 1 Plant
- Tomato 1 Fruit

- Pecans 30 Gr
- Vinegar 1 Tbsp
- White sugar 1/2 teaspoon
- Salt 1 Tbsp
- Olive oil 1 Tbsp
- Chicken Breast 100 Gr
- Garlic powder 1/2 teaspoon
- Pepper 1/2 teaspoon
- Chili powder 1/2 teaspoon

Implementation Guide

1.Chicken washed, dried. Use a knife to cut the line on the surface of the meat. Drizzle the seasoning evenly over the chicken. Bake the chicken at 175 degrees C (350 degrees F) for about 10 minutes until the chicken is cooked through. Let the chicken cool down, cut into bite-sized pieces.

2.Place lettuce, avocado and tomatoes on a plate. In a small bowl, mix 1 teaspoon vinegar, 1/2 teaspoon sugar, 2/3 teaspoon salt, 1 teaspoon olive oil. Then sprinkle evenly on the plate of vegetables. Place chicken on top. Sprinkle some pecans on top. When eating, stir it up!

Thai Shrimp Salad

Element

- Fresh shrimp 450 gr
- Lettuce 100 Gr
- Onion 1 Bulb
- Cucumber 2 Fruits
- Carrot 3 Tubers

- Purple Onion 2 Bulbs
- Mint leaves 30 Gr
- Lemongrass 1 Tree
- Bean sprouts 50 Gr
- Cooking Oil 1 Tbsp
- Lemon 2 Fruits
- Ginger 1 Bulb
- Fish sauce 30 ml
- White Sugar 15 Gr
- Chili 2 Fruits
- Garlic 1 Bulb

Implementation Guide

1.Prepare all the ingredients. Wash shrimp, peel, remove the black thread and leave the tail. Wash the sprouts, peel the carrots and cucumbers and then grate them.

2.Put the juice of 2 lemons, 30ml of fish sauce, 15g of sugar, crushed chillies, garlic and thinly sliced ginger into a small pot, bring to a boil over low heat, while stirring until the sugar dissolves completely. Then turn off the stove, filter the water, let it cool, discard the rest.

3. Lemongrass take the white head, cut into thin slices. Coriander, mint leaves washed, drained, cut into small pieces. Onions and shallots, peeled and thinly sliced.

4.Skewer the shrimp on the grill, spread a layer of cooking oil. Grill shrimp on griddle until cooked and remove from skewers.

5. Put all the vegetable ingredients in a bowl - except for the shrimp - then pour over the cooled salad dressing and mix well. Do not pour all the mixing water, but only drizzle 1/2, mix well and taste a small piece of salad, if it is enough, then stop, and if it is pale, add more.

6. Then take out the plate, put the shrimp on the surface of the salad plate, when using it, mix the shrimp well.

White Radish Salad

Element

- 2 Radish White Radish
- Green onions 100 Gr
- Chili powder 1/2 teaspoon
- White sugar 1 Tbsp
- Salt 1/2 teaspoon

- Minced Garlic 1 Tbsp
- Vinegar 2 Tbsp

Implementation Guide

1. White radish peeled, washed, using a tool to grate into long fibers. Scallions washed, cut into small pieces.

2.Put white radish in a bowl with green onion, 1/2 teaspoon paprika, 1 teaspoon white sugar, 1/2 teaspoon salt, 1 teaspoon minced garlic, 2 tablespoons vinegar, mix well .

3.The finished beet salad. Simple, fast for the whole family to use immediately with rice.

Bell pepper salad

Ingredient

- 200 grams of salad.
- 1 yellow bell pepper.
- 5 cherry tomatoes.
- 1 cucumber
- Vegetarian fish sauce, vinegar, sugar, chili.

- 4 pieces of vegetarian ribs.
- 100g roasted peanuts.
- bell pepper vegetarian salad

Making

Soak vegetables such as vegetables, melons, tomatoes, bell peppers and wash, drain.

Cut the cucumber in circles, cut the cherry tomatoes in half, and cut the bell peppers in the shape of a petal.

Soak the veggie short ribs until soft, then marinate with soy sauce, sugar, and pepper, then pan-fry, then tear into strips.

Add 1 teaspoon of sugar, 1 teaspoon of vegetarian fish sauce, ½ teaspoon of vinegar, 1 tablespoon of water and minced chili with chili sauce, and mix well.

Arrange the vegetables on a plate and drizzle the sauce evenly over the vegetables. Arrange the ribs, sprinkle with some roasted peanuts and mayonnaise.

Nutritional information of bell peppers

Bell peppers are not only an ingredient in weight loss and beauty dishes, they also provide many healthy nutrients. Specifically, in 100g of red bell pepper contains:

Calories: 31
Country: 92%
Protein: 1g
Carbs: 6g
Sugar: 4.2g
Fiber: 2.1g
Fat: 0.3g

Salad mixed with veggie tomato sauce

Ingredient

- 300g lettuce
- 100g cherry tomatoes
- 1 onion

- Young bean mold
- Boaro
- 1 piece fragrant

How to make a salad with veggie tomato sauce

Lettuce, cherry tomatoes washed. Tofu cut yarn and then fried. You grind pineapple and tomatoes to make sauce.

Put the pan on high, then saute boaro, put the molded beans and veggie spring rolls in the rim. Next, add aromatic and ground tomatoes, season to taste, and then add the young molded beans and mix well to avoid crushing the molded beans.

Put the lettuce on a plate, add cherry tomatoes and onions and drizzle the sauce over.

Tomato Salad

Ingredient

- 1 corn of salad
- 10 cherry tomatoes
- 1 white onion
- 1 cucumber

- 1 seedless lemon
- Sugar, salt, pepper

How to make tomato salad

Wash salad, tomatoes, onions with diluted salt water. Then, cut the salad, cucumber, tomato in half and then thinly slice the onion.

Squeeze the lemon juice into the onion and add 2 tablespoons of sugar and a little salt. Soak onions to absorb.

Mix salad, onions, tomatoes and sprinkle with a little pepper.

Salad Sweet Potato Bell Peppers

Ingredients:

- Sweet potato: 2 Tubers (Large)
- Coconut oil: 2 Tbsp
- Minced green onions: 3 plants

- Bell pepper: 1 Fruit
- Zucchini: 1 Fruit
- Coriander: 1/2 Cup (Minced)
- Sugar syrup: 2 Tablespoons (Maple)
- Lemon juice: 2 Tbsp
- Chili powder: 1 teaspoon
- Pepper: 1/2 teaspoon
- Salt: 1 teaspoon
- Mustard: 2 Tablespoons (Yellow)

How to make zucchini sweet potato salad:

Step 1: Preheat the oven to 190 degrees Celsius. Cut the sweet potatoes into small cubes, arrange the sweet potatoes on a baking tray, drizzle with coconut oil and pepper evenly and bake the sweet potatoes for 45-60 minutes until the sweet potatoes are soft.

Put the sweet potatoes on a plate, mix with bell peppers, diced zucchini, coriander, and chopped green onions.

Step 2: Mix sugar syrup, lime juice, yellow mustard, paprika, and pepper in a bowl until blended. Then add a cup of sauce to a bowl of vegetable salad, continue to mix well and enjoy immediately.

Mexican Purple Cabbage Salad

Ingredients for Mexican Purple Cabbage Salad:

- Purple Cabbage: 1 Pc (Large)
- Cassava root: 1 tuber
- Bell peppers: 2
- Lemon: 1 Fruit

- Horny chili: 1 Fruit (Green)
- Coriander: 50 Gr
- Carrots: 4 Tubers
- Green onions: 5 plants
- Dill powder: 3/4 teaspoon
- Coriander powder (cilantro powder): 1/2 teaspoon
- Chili powder: 1/4 teaspoon
- Honey: 1 Tbsp
- Olive oil: 3 Tablespoons
- Salt: 1 teaspoon
- Pepper: 1/2 teaspoon

How to make Mexican Purple Cabbage Salad:

Step 1:

Finely chopped purple cabbage. Bell peppers, cassava tubers, and shredded carrots. Scallions, chili peppers, chopped coriander. Place the vegetable mixture in a mixing bowl.

Step 2:

Squeeze lemon juice. Put cumin powder, coriander powder, honey, lemon juice, olive oil, chili powder, salt and pepper in a separate bowl, use a small beater to mix well.

Step 3:

When eating, you take out a little bit of the vegetable mixture and mix it with a certain amount of sauce. Before eating, to make the salad more fresh, you can put the ingredients and salad in the refrigerator 1 hour before.

Tropical Fruit Salad

Ingredients Servings:

- Lettuce 80 Gr
- Purple Lettuce 50 Gr
- Red radish 1 tuber
- Orange 1/2 Fruit

- Tropical fruit cocktail Dole 100 Gr
- Honey 3 Tbsp
- Apple Cider Vinegar 2 Tbsp
- Olive oil 1/2 teaspoon

Implementation Guide

1 Lettuce you cut off the root, soak in salt water, then wash and dry. Wash the oranges and red beets. Have a cup of Dole tropical fruit cocktail ready.

2. Stir together honey, apple cider vinegar, olive oil, a few drops of lemon juice and grate some lemon zest to create a special flavor for the salad.

3. Cut 2 types of lettuce into bite-sized pieces depending on your preference.

4. Red radish I cut into thin slices for decoration, the thinner the cut, the more beautiful it is and less pungent when eaten. I peeled the yellow oranges and carefully separated them into segments as shown in the picture.

5. Arrange 2 types of lettuce below, above are oranges, red beets and especially Dole tropical fruit cocktail with a lot of tropical fruits as diverse as pineapple, papaya, cherries, jelly coconut. Finally, just drizzle the vinegar sauce and mix the salad well!

6. Tropical fruit salad is delicious, eye-catching and very easy to eat. The ingredients seem unrelated, but when combined, they bring an irresistible flavor. What are you waiting for, if you haven't started doing it yet!

Mixed Fruit Salad

Element

- Kiwi 2 Fruits
- Pineapple 1/2 Fruit
- Ripe Mango 1 Fruit
- Strawberry 5 Fruits

- Mint leaves 4 Leaves
- Vanilla 1 Tbsp
- White sugar 1/3 teaspoon
- Lemon juice 1 Tbsp

Implementation Guide

1.Kiwi cut small pieces on top of kiwi fruit, scoop out the kiwi flesh with a spoon, keeping the skin.

2.Cut kiwi, pineapple, ripe mango, strawberry into dices. Wash mint leaves and cut into small pieces.

3. Put the mixture of fruit and mint leaves in a bowl. Add 1 teaspoon vanilla, 1/3 teaspoon white sugar, 1 teaspoon lemon juice, mix well.

4. Spoon the fruit salad mixture inside the kiwi fruit skin and enjoy!

Shrimp Fruit Salad

Element

- Fresh Shrimp200 Gr
- Apple1 Fruit
- Black Grape 100 Gr
- Cherry tomatoes100 Gr

- Lettuce 1/2 Plant
- Mayonnaise 5 Tablespoons
- Ketchup5 Tbsp
- Salt1/2 teaspoon

Implementation Guide

1. Cut off the stem of the lettuce, wash, dry and then cut into bite-sized pieces. Separate the grapes into each fruit, soak in salt water diluted with, take out to wash with clean water and dry.

Cut the apple into bite-sized pieces, remove the core. Wash cherry tomatoes, cut in half. Wash shrimp, cut off antennae, legs. Bring a pot of water to a boil, put the shrimp in to boil, then remove and peel off the shell.

2. Make salad dressing: put 5 tablespoons of mayonnaise, 5 tablespoons of ketchup, 1/2 teaspoon of salt in a medium bowl. Stir the sauce mixture thoroughly with a spoon.

Put the salad ingredients in a large bowl including lettuce, cherry tomatoes, grapes, apples, shrimp, drizzle the sauce mixture and mix well until the sauce is fully incorporated into the ingredients. Remove the salad to a plate and enjoy right away.

3. Just by making a delicious fresh shrimp fruit salad, rich in vitamin C, fiber and nutrition for the whole family's meals, more delicious and attractive than ever. In particular, this recipe also helps women take advantage of the remaining fruit resources, which is both convenient and economical, isn't it?

The salad blends the sweet and sour flavors of grapes with tomatoes and apples, with soft and chewy shrimp meat, crispy salad mixed in a fatty sauce that makes it delicious to eat without getting bored. What are you waiting for, let's not immediately save this shrimp fruit salad recipe.

Marshmallow Fruit Salad

Element

- Whipping cream226 gr
- Sour cream123 Gr
- Tangerine200 Gr

- Grapes150 GrT

- more than 200 Gr

- Grated Coconut 100 Gr

- Sponge candy200 Gr

- Cherry jam 100 Gr

- Pecans 50 Gr

Implementation Guide

1. Pineapple peeled, washed, finely chopped. Peel tangerines, separate the segments, cut in half. Wash the grapes, cut them in half, remove the seeds. Place grapes, pineapple, tangerine, grated coconut, cherry jam, marshmallows, pecans into a mixing bowl. Place in the refrigerator until use.

2. Whip whipping cream until stiff then mix with sour cream. If you're not using it right away, you can put it in the fridge. When you need to mix a salad, add a bowl of sour cream and mix it with a bowl of fruit and enjoy.

3. Marshmallow fruit salad can be eaten as a snack, for dessert or for breakfast. You can substitute any fruit you like. If you are on a weight loss diet to keep fit, you should only use unsweetened yogurt.

Mexican Fruit Salad

Element

- Pineapple 280 Gr
- Oranges 2 Fruits
- Apple 1 Fruit
- Onion 1/2 Bulb

- Lemon juice 2 Tbsp
- Coriander 1 Tbsp

Implementation Guide

1. Peel pineapple, remove the fragrant eyes, cut into small pieces to eat. Wash the apples, remove the stem, cut into thin slices, soak in water mixed with a little vinegar to not darken. Peel the onion and slice it horizontally into thin slices. Peel the orange, remove the orange peel, and remove the silk layer.

2.Put the prepared ingredients into a large bowl, add 2 tablespoons of lime juice, finely chopped coriander, mix well to use. If the spinach is more delicious, you can put this bowl of Mexican fruit salad in the refrigerator for about 1 hour and then use it!

Weight Loss Fruit Salad

Element

- Banana 1 Fruit
- Apple 1 Fruit
- Lemon 1 Fruit
- Strawberries 10 Fruits

- Blueberries 30 Fruits
- Grapes 100 Gr
- Orange 1 Fruit
- Cantaloupe 1/2 Fruit
- Grated Coconut 50 Gr

Implementation Guide

1.Prepare all ingredients. Peel banana, cut into 1.5cm thick pieces, cut in half. Wash apples, cut off the middle core, cut into bite-sized pieces. Place the sliced bananas and apples in a medium bowl.

2. Use a lemon squeezer to get water into the bowl of bananas and apples. Strawberries are washed, cut off stems, cut into bite-sized pieces. Place the cut strawberries in another bowl.

3.Next, wash and halve green grapes. Peel oranges, separate each clove, cut in half. Cantaloupe, peeled and cut into bite-sized pieces.

4.Put cantaloupe, green grapes, oranges and blueberries in a large bowl. Then add chopped strawberries and mix well. Carefully pour the bowl of banana, apple, and lemon juice into a large bowl, using a spoon to mix well. Using a spoon, carefully stir up all of the fruit.

5. Scoop the fruit into a bowl, sprinkle grated coconut on top. An eye-catching mixed fruit salad with a variety of fruit combinations is complete!

Fried Shrimp Fruit Salad

Element

- Cabbage 100 Gr
- Pomegranate 2 Fruits
- Orange 1 Fruit

- Grapes 50 Gr

- Fresh shrimp 5 pieces

- Salt 1.50 teaspoon

- Pepper 1/2 teaspoon

- Cooking oil 1 Tbsp

- Olive oil 1/2 teaspoon

- White sugar 1/4 teaspoon

- Mayonnaise 1 Tbsp

Implementation Guide

1. Young vegetables washed with salt water then drained. Peel the shrimp, cut the sugar at the back, marinate with 1 teaspoon salt, 1/2 teaspoon pepper, then use a non-stick pan for 1 teaspoon of cooking oil and bring the shrimp to the pan.

2. Pomegranate sauce: Use 1 pomegranate to squeeze the juice, add 1/2 teaspoon olive oil, 1/2 teaspoon salt and 1/4 teaspoon sugar, 1 teaspoon mayonnaise to increase flavor for the sauce.

3.Put the vegetables into a large bowl, add sliced pomegranates and oranges, grapes, and shrimp to the sauce, then use chopsticks to mix well for the vegetables to absorb the seasoning.

4. Put salad vegetables on a plate, can use more smoothies or juices when eating.

Sweet Sour Fruit Salad

Element

- Ripe Mango 1 Fruit
- Kiwi 2 Fruits
- Papaya 200 Gr

- Mint Leaves 6 Leaves
- Orange juice 60 ml
- Yogurt 2 Jars

Implementation Guide

1. Peel the mango, remove the seed, and cut it into dices. Cut the papaya in half, scoop out the seeds with a spoon, cut it into small pieces, and put it in a bowl of mango.

2.Kiwi cut in half horizontally, use a spoon to scoop out the intestines, cut pomegranate seeds, put in a bowl of mango, papaya.

3. Wash mint leaves, cut into small pieces, put in the fruit bowl in step 2, mix well.

4.Finally, add 60ml of orange juice, mix well to blend the fruit together.

5.Put the salad into a bowl or cup, add yogurt and you're done. You can eat it with rice paper!

Fruit Salad with Orange Sauce

Element

- Ripe Mango 2 Fruits
- Papaya 1 Fruit
- Kiwi 3 Fruits

- 3 leaves mint leaves
- Orange juice 70 ml

Implementation Guide

1. Mango peeled, diced to taste. Papayas and kiwis are also peeled and diced (remember to remove the seeds). Mint leaves chopped. Put all the fruit in a large bowl, drizzle the orange juice over and mix well until the fruit soaks up the sauce.

2. Put the fruit salad on a plate or small bowl and let your baby enjoy it.

Summer Fruit Salad

Element

- Tangerine 2 Fruits
- Grapes 300 Gr
- Blueberries 100 Gr
- Strawberry 150 Gr

- Pineapple 1/2 Fruit
- Raspberries 100 Gr
- Mint leaves 5 Leaves
- Honey 170 Gr
- Lemon 1 Fruit
- Orange1 Left

Implementation Guide

1. Make the sauce: Put 170g of honey, orange juice, and lemon juice in a bowl, stir until the mixture is even. Strawberries washed, cut into bite-sized pieces. Raspberries, blueberries, grapes washed and drained. Pineapple peeled, diced medium. Split orange.

2.Put everything into a large bowl, pour in the prepared sauce, mix well until the fruit absorbs all the sauce. Add mint leaves to create fragrance and add beauty.

3.Put the summer fruit salad on a deep plate and enjoy.

Rum Fruit Salad

Element

- Oranges 4 Fruits
- Pineapple 1/2 Fruit
- Kiwi 2 Fruits
- Ripe Mango 2 Fruits

- Rum 3 Tablespoons
- Honey 2 Tbsp

Implementation Guide

1. Peel the oranges, then separate the segments, remove the seeds. Peel kiwi and mango, wash and cut into small squares. Peel the pineapple, remove the eyes, wash and cut as fragrant. Put all the fruit in a bowl.

2.Put the bowl of fruit into the fridge for 1-2 hours to cool. When you need to use, you take out the fruit bowl, mix the rum with honey and mix again, pour into the bowl to mix well. so you can enjoy it.

3.Rum fruit salad is a quick and simple dish, used for dessert or can be used in family meals, barbecue parties. With eye-catching colors like this, no matter how hot the summer is, it's instantly cool.

Fruit Salad with Lemon Sauce

Element

- Pineapple 1/2 Fruit
- Strawberry 100 Gr
- Raspberries 170 Gr

- Blueberries 85 Gr
- Ripe Mango 1 Fruit
- Lemon 1/2 Fruit

Implementation Guide

1. Strawberries washed, cut into bite-sized pieces. Pineapple, peeled mango, cut into squares. Raspberries (black and red), blueberries washed, drained. Put all the fruit in a glass bowl, add the grated lemon zest and squeeze out the juice of 1/2 lemon. Mix well and you're done.

2.Place the salad on a plate and enjoy. Fruit salad with lemon sauce is cool, rich in fiber and is the most effective weight loss food.

Fruit Salad with Honey Sauce

Element

- Grapes 140 Gr
- Mulberry 100 Gr
- Watermelon 300 Gr

- Cantaloupe 340Gr
- Watermelon 450 Gr
- Coconut Oil 5 Tbsp
- Lemon 1 Fruit
- Honey5 Tbsp

Implementation Guide

1.Fruits are washed and dried. Peel and finely chop the melons and melons. Add the fruits and mixing bowl and refrigerate before serving. Make honey sauce: mix coconut oil, honey, lemon juice in another bowl.

2. When using, you put honey sauce in the fruit bowl, mix well and enjoy. Fruit is always a great assistant to help you lose weight or beautify. The bowl of mixed fruit is cool, the flavors of the mixed fruits create a very delicious taste.

White Wine Fruit Salad

Element

- Wine 250 ml
- White Sugar 85 Gr
- Strawberry 400 Gr
- Cantaloupe 200 Gr

- Blueberries 300 Gr
- Mint leaves 8 Leaves

Implementation Guide

1.Put 85g of white sugar, 250ml of white wine into a pot, cook on the stove until the sugar dissolves, then turn off the heat and let it cool. Strawberries cut into bite-sized pieces. Peel the cucumber and cut it into squares. Blueberries washed, drained. Minced mint leaves.

2. Put the fruits in a large glass bowl with mint leaves and drizzle the wine mixture over. Mix well and you can enjoy.

3.Fruit salad mixed with aromatic wine, a bit mild, sweet and sour fruit brings a delicious feeling.

Fruit Salad Cream Cheese

Element

- Cream cheese 226 gr
- White Sugar 100 Gr
- Vanilla essence 1/2 teaspoon

- Strawberry 100 Gr
- Kiwi 100 Gr
- Ripe Mango 100 Gr
- Fragrant 100 Gr
- Whipping cream 4 Tbsp

Implementation Guide

1. Leave the cream cheese at room temperature to soften. Whipping cream whip until it forms a peak. Beat cream cheese for about 2 minutes, add sugar and vanilla essence, beat until softened. Add whipping cream and mix gently. Place the bowl of cheese in the refrigerator.

2. Strawberries are washed and cut into small pieces. Mango, pineapple, kiwi peeled, diced. Put mango, pineapple, kiwi in a mixing bowl. Place the bowl of fruit in the refrigerator until ready to use.

3. When eating, you put the bowl of cream cheese into the bowl of fruit and mix well. This dish can be used as a dessert, served with bread, or as a cake frosting.

Fruit Salad with Passionfruit Sauce

Element

- Fresh tiger prawns 3-5 pieces
- 1 apple
- Dragon fruit 1 fruit
- Avocado 1 fruit

- Passion fruit 1 fruit
- Mayonnaise, Honey
- Decorative coriander

Implementation Guide

1.Dragon fruit, apple, avocado cut into small squares to eat. Shrimp peeled, head, tail washed. Marinated in shrimp 1/4 teaspoon salt, 1/4 teaspoon chili powder, 1 pinch of ground pepper.

Note: Apples, after cutting, should be soaked in cold water with a little salt to prevent the apples from turning brown. Avocados should choose ripe to not overripe fruit, which will make the avocado soft and difficult to cut.

2.Put the pan on the stove, put 1 tablespoon of cooking oil in the pan, and then fry the shrimp on both sides. The red cooked shrimp is slightly browned, then take it out for a plate

3. Mix sauce: Put 1 tablespoon of mayonnaise in the bowl, the inside of 1 passion fruit, take the seeds, followed by 1/2 teaspoon of honey. Stirred

4.Place the fruit on a plate and add shrimp on top. Drizzle the dressing evenly on top, garnish with cilantro to make it beautiful. Finished: Salad with fresh fruit and sweet shrimp. Combined with strange sweet and sour passion fruit sauce. This will be a salad with lots of vitamins and few calories

Tropical Fruit Salad with Honey Sauce

Element

- Starfruit 1 Fruit
- Kiwi 1 Fruit
- Orange 1 Fruit
- Strawberries 4 Fruits

- Tangerine 2 Fruits

- Ginger 1 Piece

- Honey 1/4 Cup

- Lemon 1/4 Fruit

- Horny chili 1 Fruit

Implementation Guide

1. Wash the star fruit and strawberries. Peel off the 2 ends and 5 edges of the star fruit. Remove the stalks of the strawberries and cut them into pieces. 4. Peel the oranges and tangerines, separate the segments, and remove the seeds. Peel the kiwi and cut it into small squares. Put all the fruit in a bowl.

2. Wash, remove seeds and finely chop the horn peppers. Peel a thumb-sized piece of ginger and grate it. Grate the zest of 1/4 lemon and squeeze out the juice. Put lemon zest, lime juice, grated ginger, and honey together in a bowl. Pour the bowl of mixed sauce into the fruit bowl and mix well.

3. Tropical fruit salad with honey sauce is a quick and simple dish, used for breakfast or can be used in family meals, barbecue parties. In addition, if the children refuse to eat fruit, the colorful eye-catching salad bowl above is also an effective form of temptation.

Cauliflower Salad
with Dragonfly Caviar

Element

- Spinach 200 Gr
- Sprouts 100 Gr
- Orange 1 Fruit
- Kiwi 1 Fruit

- Salmon 50 Gr
- Caviar 30 Gr
- Mustard 1/2 teaspoon
- Mayonnaise 1 teaspoon

Implementation Guide

1. Peel the yellow orange, slice it thinly to taste (leave 1/3 of the fruit for the sauce). Kiwi peeled, cut round, thin about 0.3 - 0.5 cm. Wash the sprouts and pat dry. Cauliflower washed, cut into bite-sized pieces.

2. Mix salad dressing with 1 teaspoon of mayonnaise, 1/2 teaspoon of yellow mustard, 1 teaspoon of flying fish roe and 30 ml of orange juice, beat until well blended into a sauce.

3. Arrange vegetables and fruits in bowls or plates, add thinly sliced fresh salmon sashimi and beautiful flying fish roe.

4. When serving, drizzle the sauce over the face and mix well. You can put the salad in the fridge 15 minutes before serving to make the salad more crispy! Good luck!

Quinoa Fruit Salad

Element

- Quinoa 200 Gr
- Blueberries 100 Gr
- Strawberry 100 Gr
- Ripe Mango 1 Fruit

- Cantaloupe 1/2 Fruit

- Basil 20 Gr

- Honey 85 Gr

- Lemon 1 Fruit

Implementation Guide

1.Put the quinoa seeds into a pot with water and cook until soft. Put 85g of honey, lemon juice in a bowl and mix well. Blueberries, washed strawberries, chopped strawberries.

Mango, cantaloupe peeled, cut into pieces. Then, place the cooked quinoa in a large bowl with the chopped fruit and basil and mix well. Finally, pour in the prepared sauce and mix well.

2.Quinoa fruit salad is extremely simple with cool, sour, sweet and fresh flavors and fresh fruits to bring a beautiful skin, a healthy body. What are housewives waiting for without quickly saving the recipe.

Purple cabbage salad

Ingredient

- ½ purple cabbage.
- 1 cucumber.
- carrot
- 3 tablespoons roasted sesame sauce

How to make purple cabbage salad

Cut the purple cabbage into thin strands and then wash with water until no more purple color, take out and drain.

Wash cucumber, cut into bite-sized pieces and remove seeds.
Wash the carrots, cut them into thin slices.

Put all the vegetables in a bowl, add some roasted sesame sauce and mix well, let it sit for about 30 minutes and you can enjoy it.
purple cabbage vegetarian salad

Nutritional information of purple cabbage
Although not many calories, purple cabbage contains many nutrients that are good for health.

According to experts, in 89g of cabbage includes:

Calories: 28

Protein: 1g

Carbs: 7g

Fiber: 2g

Vitamin C: 56%

Vitamin K: 28%

Vitamin B6: 11%

Vitamin A: 6%

Potassium: 5%

Thiamine: 5%

Riboflavin: 5%

Besides, purple cabbage also provides a small amount of substances such as iron, calcium, magnesium, copper, zinc

Salad mixed with tomato sauce

Ingredient

- 300g lettuce.
- 100g cherry tomatoes.
- 1 onion.
- Young bean mold.

- Onions
- 1 piece fragrant.

How to make a salad with veggie tomato sauce

Wash lettuce and cherry tomatoes. Molded bean curd cut into strands to eat and then fried. Pineapple and tomato puree to make sauce.

Put the pan on the stove, add the onion to the pan and fry until fragrant, then put the molded beans and vegetarian rolls into the stock.

Next, add the aromatic mixture and the pureed tomatoes. Season to taste, turn off the heat and add the molded beans to the mix. Mix gently to avoid crushing the beans and you're done with the vegetarian tomato salad.

Vegan avocado salad

Ingredient

- 2 avocados
- 1 cucumber
- 500g tomatoes
- 1/2 purple onion

- 2 tablespoons olive oil
- 2 tablespoons fresh lemon juice
- Coriander
- Salt
- Pepper

How to make vegan avocado salad

Wash cucumber, tomato, red onion, cut into thin slices.
Peel avocado, diced.

Chop the tomatoes, cucumber, red onion, and chopped avocado in a large bowl.

Next, add 2 tablespoons of olive oil, 2 tablespoons of fresh lemon juice to the salad and mix well. Finally, put the salad on a plate, add a little salt and pepper and enjoy.

Note: You should choose avocados with green skin, yellow dots. Because these fruits will have a softer and fatter core than purple avocados. And elongated avocados are always tastier than round avocados because their seeds are smaller and contain more kernels.

Nutritional information of avocado

In 100g avocado contains many healthy nutrients such as:

Vitamin K: 26%

Folate: 20%

Vitamin C: 17%

Potassium: 14%

Vitamin B5: 14%

Vitamin B6: 13%

Vitamin E: 10%

Vegetarian seaweed salad

Ingredient

- 15g dried seaweed
- 100g lettuce frise
- 100g purple loto lettuce

- 1 orange
- 20g white sugar
- 1g black sesame
- 2 teaspoons apple cider vinegar
- 4 teaspoons sesame oil
- 2 tablespoons soy sauce.
- Vegetarian seaweed salad

Making

Soak seaweed in water for about 15 minutes to bloom evenly, then wash and drain.

Peel oranges, separate oranges into small segments, set aside.

Remove the old leaves of frise and purple lolo lettuce, soak in salted water for about 15 minutes, then take out, wash and drain.

Place the soy sauce, sugar, apple cider vinegar, and sesame oil in a small bowl and stir until the sugar dissolves.

Prepare a large bowl, put seaweed, lettuce in and pour the sauce made and mix it all.

Finally, you put the orange slices on top, sprinkle a few more roasted sesame seeds and you're done with the vegetarian seaweed salad.

When eating, you will feel a little bitterness of the salad, then soothed by the sweet and sour taste of the sauce mixture. The aroma of roasted sesame makes the dish more attractive.

Nutritional information of seaweed
Seaweed contains more minerals, trace elements and other nutrients than other foods.

In 100g of seaweed, there are the following nutrients:

Carbs: 10g

Protein: 2g

Fat: 1g

Optical fiber: 35%

Magnesium: 180%I

Vitamin K: 80%

Manganese: 70%

Iodine: 65%

Sodium: 70%

Calcium: 60%

Folate: 50%

Potassium: 45%

Iron: 20%

Besides, seaweed also contains a small amount of nutrients such as: omega-3 and omega-6 fatty acids, vitamins A, C, E, phosphorus, vitamin B and choline.

Vegetarian sprouted salad

Ingredient

- Carrots: 50g
- Sprouts: 150g
- Purple cabbage: 100g
- Grapes: 5 fruits

- Straw mushroom: 100g
- Cherry tomatoes: 6
- Tofu: 1 piece
- Vegetarian spring rolls: 1 piece
- Mayonnaise, olive oil, apple cider vinegar
- Pepper, chili, garlic
- sprouted vegetarian salad

Making

Wash carrots, peel and cut into thin strips. Cut the purple cabbage into thin slices, cut into thin slices or thin strips to taste.

Wash sprouts and cherry tomatoes, drain.

Choose fresh straw mushrooms, cut off the heads and wash them thoroughly.

Wash the tofu and cut it into thin slices.

Put a pan on the stove, add oil, then add vegetarian rolls, mushrooms and tofu and stir-fry. Season to taste and stir-fry until fully cooked.

Sauté garlic and chili, then drain the oil and keep it separate.

Make sauce with sauteed garlic, 2 tablespoons mayonnaise, 1 tablespoon sugar, 1 tablespoon apple cider vinegar, 1/5 teaspoon pepper and garlic oil, mix well.

Put all the ingredients in a large bowl including: carrots, sprouts, purple cabbage, grapes, cherry tomatoes, sauteed mushroom mix, tofu and vegetarian spring rolls. Then, you proceed to mix well, pour the sauce over and enjoy.

Watermelon Salad

Element

- Watermelon 1/2 Fruit
- Cucumber 1 Fruit
- Raspberry 50 Gr
- Onion 1 Bulb
- Olives 25 Gr

- Wine 1 Tbsp
- Lemon 1/2 Fruit
- Mustard 1/2 Tbsp
- Cheese 20 Gr
- Mint leaves 10 Gr
- Salt 1/2 teaspoon
- Pepper 1/2 teaspoon

Implementation Guide

1.Raspberries washed, put in a blender, puree. Then put in a separate cup.

2.Next add the mustard to the bowl of freshly ground raspberries, plus the red wine. Squeeze a little fresh lemon into the cup, sprinkle with pepper and beat well.

3. Wash mint leaves, cut into small pieces. Then put in the raspberry sauce. Mix up.

4. Chop melons, olives, onions, cheese. Same size.

5.Put everything in a bowl, sprinkle with salt and pour in the raspberry sauce and mix together. And finally enjoy.

Strawberry Watermelon Salad

Element

- Strawberries 12 Fruits
- Watermelon 1/2 Fruit
- Basil 6 Leaves
- Honey 2 Tbsp

Implementation Guide

1.Prepare raw fish. Strawberries washed, drained, diced.

2.Watermelon seedless, diced. Basil leaves are washed and finely chopped.

3. Put strawberries, watermelon in a bowl, sprinkle minced basil leaves on top, drizzle 2 tablespoons of honey and mix well.

4.So the strawberry watermelon salad is ready! Not only delicious, cool but also good for health.

Yogurt Watermelon Salad

Element

- Watermelon 300 Gr
- Coconut Oil 2 Tbsp
- Fresh rosemary leaves 10 gr

- Honey 1 Tbsp
- Yogurt 250 Gr
- Lemon 1/2 Fruit
- Salt 2 Tbsp
- Pepper 2 Tbsp

Implementation Guide

1.Heat a pan with coconut oil, add rosemary leaves to the island for 1 minute until fragrant, then take it out and put it in a bowl. Watermelon cut into bite-sized pieces. In a large bowl, mix honey and yogurt until smooth.

In a small bowl, mix together salt and pepper. Ladle yogurt onto a plate, top with watermelon, sprinkle with fried rosemary leaves in the oil and squeeze the juice of 1/2 lemon. Finally add the salt and pepper mixture and you're done.

2. Now you just have to enjoy the delicious, refreshing yogurt watermelon salad. Hurry up and save this delicious and strange salad recipe right away, it's sure to be great.

Strawberry Beet Salad

Element

- Beets 700 Gr
- Strawberry 300 Gr
- Green Onion 1 Plant
- Olive Oil 3 Tbsp

- Vinegar 1 Tbsp
- Salt 1/2 teaspoon
- Pepper 1/4 teaspoon
- Watercress Salad 200 Gr

Implementation Guide

1.Beets peeled, washed, cut into medium pieces. Hand-wash strawberries, remove stems, cut in half. Open the oven at 200 degrees C. Put the beets on a baking tray, drizzle with olive oil and a little pepper, salt, mix well, then put in the oven for 60 - 70 minutes until soft, then remove.

2.Put the beets into a bowl with the strawberries, scallions and drizzle with olive oil, vinegar and salt, mix well and that's it. When eating, put the salad on a plate, add lettuce, hemp seeds on top and just enjoy.

3.Raspberry beetroot salad with natural sweetness accompanied by a little sourness of strawberries and spices, all blended together to create an irresistible delicious taste. Those of you who want to lose weight, quickly save this recipe right away.

Chia Seed Vinegar Salad

Element

- Strawberries 2 Cups
- Lettuce 2 Cups
- Oats 2 Tbsp
- Dried Coconut 1/4 Cup

- Pecans 1/2 Cup
- Cheese i3 Tbsp
- Olive oil 1/4 Cup
- Red Vinegar 3 Tbsp
- Honey 1 Tbsp
- Chia seeds 2 teaspoons

Implementation Guide

1.Wash the zucchini, remove the stalk, and cut it into small pieces. Lettuce, washed and sliced. Place strawberries, lettuce, pecans, oats, desiccated coconut, cheese in a separate bowl. Mix all ingredients in Chia Seed Sauce together in a separate bowl.

2. You sprinkle the chia seed sauce evenly over the salad bowl and mix well, put in the refrigerator for about 1 hour before serving. Put the salad on a plate, it looks very attractive, isn't it?

Strawberry Chicken Salad

Element

- Chicken 2 Chicken
- Lettuce 200 Gr
- Strawberry 250 Gr
- Olive Oil 3 Tbsp

- Vinegar 3 Tbsp
- Lemon1 Fruit
- Honey 1 Tbsp
- White Sesame 1 Tbsp
- Salt 1/2 teaspoon
- Pepper 1/2 teaspoon

Implementation Guide

1. Make lemon honey vinegar oil: Squeeze the juice of 1 lemon into a cup, add 1 tablespoon olive oil, 1 tablespoon vinegar, 1 teaspoon honey, 1 teaspoon roasted white sesame. Mix all the spices together.

2.In another cup put 2 tablespoons olive oil, 2 tablespoons vinegar, mix well.

3. Wash chicken breast, marinate chicken breast with salt and pepper. Then put in a cup of olive oil and vinegar to soak for about 15 minutes for the meat to infuse the spices. Then add the chicken and cook until cooked through.

4. Lettuce and raspberries washed, strawberries cut off the stem. Cut the above 2 ingredients into small pieces. Put strawberries and lettuce in a bowl, add vinegar, honey, lemon, and mix well.

5.Finally, when the chicken is cooked, cut the grilled chicken breast and place it on top of the vegetables! Now just enjoy the strawberry chicken salad!

Orange Salad

Element

- Oranges 2 Fruits
- Apple 1 Fruit
- Fresh Shrimp 100 Gr
- Mustard 1 Tbsp

- Salt 1 Tbsp
- White Sugar 1 Tbsp
- Pepper 1/2 teaspoon
- Lemon juice 1 Tbsp

Implementation Guide

1.Cut the avocado in half, remove the seed, use a spoon to scoop out the avocado flesh. Cut the orange in half, remove all the orange cloves, leave the peel for garnish.

2. Apples are washed, cut into small pieces, squares. Then, put apples, oranges, and avocados in a bowl.

3. Shrimp washed, peeled, removed head and tail and then boiled. Put shrimp in the bowl of avocado, apple, orange. Add 1 teaspoon of mustard, 1 teaspoon of salt, white sugar, pepper, and 1 tablespoon of lemon juice, mix well.

4. Put the salad in the orange peel to make the dish more attractive and beautiful. Add it to your home menu to combat boredom!

Aniseed Orange Salad

Element

- Anise root 200 Gr
- Oranges 5 Fruits
- Onion 1 Bulb
- Lemon 1/2 Fruit

- Orange juice 20 ml
- Salt 1 Tbsp
- Pepper 1/4 teaspoon
- Olive Oil 3 Tbsp

Implementation Guide

1. Orange peeled, sliced thin. Peel anise, wash, cut into thin slices to taste. Sliced onion. Chahh squeeze the water. Put the onion in a bowl, sprinkle with lemon juice, mix well for 10 minutes. Then put anise, orange on a plate, sprinkle with pepper, salt, orange juice, olive oil and mix well. Then add the onion and mix again to enjoy.

2.When eating, you can sprinkle more cilantro or the leaves of anise to create fragrance. Try this very simple way of making anise orange salad with delicious taste as well as extremely beneficial for health.

Sweet and Sour Orange Salad

Element

- Oranges 2 Fruits
- Honey 1 Tbsp
- Lemon juice 1 Tbsp
- 3 leaves mint leaves

Implementation Guide

1. Mix 1 tablespoon honey, 1 tablespoon lemon juice. Peel oranges, cut into thin slices. Arrange each orange slice on a plate, drizzle honey lemon juice on top, sprinkle with finely chopped mint leaves and you're done.

2. Now you just have to enjoy this delicious, sweet and sour salad. On hot days or you are looking to lose weight, supplement with vitamin C, save this sweet and sour orange salad recipe, it will taste great.

Thai-style Spicy Dried Shrimp Salad

Element

- Orange 3 Fruits
- Coriander 10 Gr
- Chili 2 Fruits

- Peanuts 10 Gr

- Dried Shrimp 10 Gr

- Horny chili 1 Fruit

- Garlic 1 Bulb

- Purple Onion 2 Bulbs

- White Sugar 3 Tablespoons

- Tamarind juice 3 Tbsp

- Fish sauce 3 Tbsp

- Lemon leaves 2 Leaves

Implementation Guide

1.Put into a food processor including: finely chopped horny chili, peeled garlic, peeled red onion, finely chopped lime leaves, 3 tablespoons sugar, 3 tablespoons fish sauce and 3 tablespoons tamarind juice, Turn on the machine and puree it into a salad mix.

2. Peel the oranges, remove the layers and seeds, and chop the oranges into a bowl. Add to the mixture just ground, roasted peanuts and dried shrimp, chopped chili, mix well. Depending on your taste, increase or decrease the amount of salad dressing! For me, about 3 tablespoons of mixed sauce is enough.

Watermelon
Blueberry Salad

Element

- Watermelon 600 Gr
- Blueberries 200 Gr
- Mint leaves 20 Gr

- Olive Oil 2 Tbsp

- Vinegar 1 Tbsp

- Lemon juice 2 Tbsp

- Lemon Peel 1 Slice

- Pepper 1/4 teaspoon

- Salt 1/4 teaspoon

- Cheese 50 Gr

Implementation Guide

1.Cut watermelon into bite-sized pieces. Blueberries washed. In a small bowl, mix together 2 tablespoons of olive oil, 1 tablespoon of vinegar, 2 tablespoons of lemon juice, finely chopped mint leaves, salt and pepper, and grated lemon zest. Put the watermelon and blueberries in a large bowl, pour the sauce over and mix well and you're done.

2. When serving the salad on a deep plate, sprinkle more cheese on top with mint leaves and enjoy. Sweet and cool blueberry watermelon salad helps you both lose weight and cool off effectively. Quickly save the recipe right away.

Watermelon Vegetable Salad

Element

- Watermelon 1/4 Fruit
- Cucumber 2 Fruits
- Onion 1/2 Bulb
- Lemon juice 30 ml

- Mint leaves 10 Gr
- Coconut milk 50 ml
- Olive oil 50 ml

Implementation Guide

1.Sauce: put 50ml of coconut milk, 50ml of olive oil, 30ml of lemon juice in a bowl and stir well. Peel the watermelon and cut it into squares. Wash cucumber, cut into cubes, thinly slice onion. Mint leaves washed and finely chopped.

Put the watermelon, cucumber and onion in a bowl with the silver leaves, drizzle the sauce on top and mix well. If you don't eat it right away, put it in the fridge. When eating, just sprinkle more silver leaves and enjoy.

2.Watermelon vegetable salad with many sources of nutrients and suitable for those who are in the process of dieting and losing weight. Don't hesitate to save the recipe right away, the taste is guaranteed to be delicious.

Strawberry Salad

Element

- Bacon 8 Slices
- Lettuce 50 Gr
- Cheese 180 Gr
- Cucumber 50 Gr
- Strawberries 12 Fruits

- Olive Oil 5 Tbsp

- Vinegar 2 Tbsp

- Spend 1 Tbsp

- Salt 1 Tbsp

- Avocado 1 Fruit

- Pecans 50 Gr

Implementation Guide

1. Bake or re-fry bacon until brown. Cut into bite-sized pieces.

2. Cheese cut into small pieces. Strawberries washed, cut into quarters. Cucumbers are washed and cut into small pieces. Square cut butter.

3.Mix olive oil, vinegar, salt and pepper together. Place all the lettuce, strawberries, bacon, and pecans in a large bowl, pour in the olive oil mixture and mix well. This dish is delicious to eat or eat with grilled dishes!

Strawberry Apple Salad

Element

- Strawberry 200 Gr
- Grapcs 50 Gr
- Apple 1 Fruit

- Orange 1 Fruit
- Yogurt 1 Jar

Implementation Guide

1.Bought strawberries, washed and then soaked in dilute salt water for about 5 minutes.

2. Next, take out the strawberries, wash them again with water and then dry them. Peel apples cut into bite-sized pieces, remember to soak them in salt water to prevent the apples from turning black! Peel the oranges and then cut them into bite-sized pieces.

3.Put oranges, strawberries, apples, raisins in a bowl. Pour yogurt over and mix well. The amount of yogurt depends on your taste! You can put the salad in the refrigerator to eat better.

Orange Avocado Salad

Element

- Lettuce 300 Gr
- Avocado 1 Fruit
- Orange 1 Fruit
- Cherry tomatoes 50 Gr

- Orange juice 60 ml
- Honey 2 Tbsp
- Vinegar 2 Tbsp
- Olive oil 1 Tbsp
- Chia seeds 1 Tbsp

Implementation Guide

1. Orange peeled, cut into slices 1cm thick, then cut orange slices into 4. Cherry tomatoes cut into 4.

2.Cut the avocado in half, remove the skin, then cut into slices 1cm thick. Arrange avocados, oranges and tomatoes on a separate plate.

3. Make salad dressing: put in a bowl 60ml of orange juice, 2 tablespoons of vinegar, 2 tablespoons of honey, 1 tablespoon of olive oil, 1 tablespoon of chia seeds and stir well.

4. Arrange the lettuce below, you can use any type of salad you can find such as batch, frise, carol or oak leaf,... In this recipe Cooky uses 300g of oak lettuce. leaf. Add sliced avocado, orange slices and cherry tomatoes on top, finally drizzle with chia seed orange sauce, mix well and enjoy.

5. Orange avocado salad is like a symphony of tropical vegetables, eye-catching color but also really delicious taste. The salad is very suitable for making a mid-afternoon snack, satisfying your hungry stomach while still being healthy and not causing weight gain, in addition to having beautiful skin effects. Save the recipe and do it

Carrot Salad

Element

- Carrot 2 Tubers
- Avocado 1 Fruit
- Onion 1/2 Bulb
- Tuna 1 Box

- Pepper 1/2 teaspoon
- Salt 1.20 teaspoon
- Sesame Oil 1 Tbsp
- Parsley 2 Branches

Implementation Guide

1. Carrots are washed, peeled and grated into thin strands. Thinly sliced onions. Put everything in a bowl, sprinkle with 1 teaspoon of salt, mix well and let it sit for about 30 minutes.

2.After 30 minutes, the carrots and onions are out of water. Place in a towel, wring out the water and place in a mixing bowl.

3. Peel avocado, cut into small squares to eat.

4.Put the cut avocado into a bowl of carrots, open the can of marinated tuna, drain off the oil from the can and put it in a bowl of carrots and butter. Season with 1/2 teaspoon pepper and 1 tablespoon sesame oil. Use a fork and spoon to mix well.

5.Cut the parsley finely and put it in a bowl of salad to mix well, season with 1/4 teaspoon salt to taste.

6. Arrange on a plate and enjoy.

French Carrot Salad

Element

- It is 100 Gr
- Parsley 100 Gr
- Salt 1/2 teaspoon
- Pepper 1/2 teaspoon

- Lemon juice 1 Tbsp
- Minced Garlic 1 Tbsp
- Olive Oil 2 Tbsp
- Carrot 2 Tubers

Implementation Guide

1. Dill leaves are chopped, the tubers are thinly grated.

2. Cut dill leaves, put in a bowl with chopped parsley, 1/2 teaspoon salt, 1/2 teaspoon pepper, 1 tablespoon lemon juice, 1 teaspoon minced garlic, 2 tablespoons olive oil soup, stir well.

3. Shredded carrots, put in a bowl. Add the mixture dissolved in step 2, mix well.

4. Put the dish on a plate and enjoy! Easy to do, easy to do, isn't it?

White Radish Carrot Salad

Element

- White radish 1 Radish
- Carrot 1 Tuber
- Chili 2 Fruits

- White Sugar 1 Tbsp

- Rice Vinegar 1 Tbsp

- Sesame Oil 1 Tbsp

- White Sesame 1 Tbsp

Implementation Guide

1.White radish, carrot peeled, washed. Use a knife to cut into long strands to eat or cut. Chopped chili. Sauce: put 1 tablespoon of sugar, 1 tablespoon of sesame oil, 1 tablespoon of rice vinegar, 1 tablespoon of roasted sesame in a cup, stir well.

1.Add white radish, grated carrot and pour the sauce on top, mix thoroughly with chopsticks to fully absorb the ingredients.

2. White radish, peeled carrots, washed. Use a knife to cut into long strands to eat or cut. Chopped chili. Sauce: put 1 tablespoon of sugar, 1 tablespoon of sesame oil, 1 tablespoon of rice vinegar, 1 tablespoon of roasted sesame in a cup, stir well.

Add white radish, grated carrot and pour the sauce on top, mix thoroughly with chopsticks to fully absorb the ingredients.

3. The white radish carrot salad is made quickly and deliciously with the crispy, sweet and sour taste that makes the meal even more delicious. What are you waiting for without quickly saving the recipe.

Carrot Tomato Salad

Element

- Carrot 2 Tubers
- Onion 1/2 Bulb
- Tomato 1 Fruit
- Pecans 6 Berries
- Cheese 50 Gr

- Vinegar 1.50 Tbsp
- Olive Oil 3 Tbsp
- Mustard 1 Tbsp
- White Sugar 1/2 Tbsp
- Carrot juice 2 Tbsp
- Salt 1/2 teaspoon
- Pepper 1/2 teaspoon

Implementation Guide

1. Peel carrots, wash, cut into 6cm long strips and rinse with cold water again. Wash tomatoes, cut into 8 small pieces. Crush pecans, place in a pan without oil and stir for 1-2 minutes.

2.You put all the ingredients for the sauce including: 1.5 tbsp vinegar, 3 tbsp olive oil, 1 tbsp mustard, ½ tbsp sugar, 2 tbsp carrot puree, 1 tbsp onion puree , a little salt, a little pepper in the bowl stir well.

Next, you put the washed greens on the plate. Place 8 pieces of tomatoes around, place the shredded carrots in the center of the plate on top of the vegetables.

3. Next, sprinkle mozzarela cheese and fried pecans on top. Finally, use a spoon to scoop the sauce over the carrots and sprinkle some pecans on top.

4. The salad plate with orange carrot, tomato red color stands out on the green color of vegetables.

Broccoli Carrot Salad

Element

- Cheese 400 Gr
- Onion 1 Bulb
- 1 bell pepper
- 4 Tubers Carrots

- Mayonnaise Sauce 200 Gr
- White Sugar 100 Gr
- Broccoli 500 Gr
- Vinegar 3 Tbsp

Implementation Guide

1. Carrots peeled, washed, cut into small pieces. Small grated cheese. Wash bell peppers and cut into small pieces.

2. Onion peeled, diced. Cauliflower, de-stemmed, washed, cut into bite-sized pieces.

3. Beat 200g of mayonnaise with 100g of white sugar and 3 tablespoons of vinegar until the sugar dissolves into a homogeneous mixture.

4. Mix carrot, broccoli, onion, bell pepper in a large bowl. Add the sauce and grated cheese mixture and mix well.

5. Arrange on a plate and enjoy.

Bell Pepper Carrot Salad

Element

- Carrots 283 Gr
- 1 bell pepper
- Horny chili pepper 1 Fruit

- Coriander 50 Gr
- Lemon 1 Fruit
- Olive Oil 3 Tbsp
- Salt 1 Tbsp
- Dill Powder 1/4 teaspoon

Implementation Guide

1.Carrots, bell peppers cleaned and sliced. Cut the green chili pepper in half, remove the seeds and core, and then chop finely. Finely chopped cilantro. Squeeze lemon juice and mix with olive oil, salt, cumin powder, and pepper in a small bowl. Mix all ingredients and sauce together.

2.Place the carrot and bell pepper salad on a plate and enjoy. With a few simple everyday ingredients, together with some spices make the dish has an unforgettable taste. If you haven't tried it yet, do it!

Mango Salad

Element

- Ripe Mango 2 Fruits
- Onion 1/4 Bulb
- Coriander 1/4 Cup
- Lemon 1/2 Fruit

- Salt 1/2 teaspoon

Implementation Guide

1. Peel the mango, scrape the flesh, and diced it. Minced purple onion. Wash and finely chop coriander. Squeeze lemon juice. Mix the mango, purple onion, minced cilantro, salt, and lemon juice together.

2. That's it, the super-fast mango salad is done. You can share this salad with grilled dishes or braised and fried dishes, ensuring that the rice will be all over because of its delicious taste.

Pinapple Mango Salad

Element

- Ripe Mango 1 Fruit
- Pineapple 1 Fruit
- Horny chili 1 Fruit
- Onion 1 Bulb

- Lemon 1 Fruit
- Coriander 3 Branches
- Salt and pepper 1/3 teaspoon

Implementation Guide

1. Peel pineapple, remove core and eyes, cut pomegranate seeds. Peel the mango, cut the pomegranate into small pieces.

2. Chopped onion and horn pepper with similar aroma and mango. Finely chopped coriander.

3.Put the mango, pineapple, onion and coriander into a bowl. Sprinkle with 1/3 teaspoon of salt and pepper, sprinkle with lemon juice and stir well.

4. Garnish the plate and wake up. There is a card to serve with baked rice paper if you like!

Avocado Mango Salad

Element

- Ripe Mango 2 Fruits
- Avocado 1 Fruit
- Minced purple onion 1/4 Cup
- Coriander 1/4 Cup

- Olive Oil 2 Tbsp
- Salt 1 Tbsp
- Chili powder 1/2 teaspoon
- Lemon 1 Fruit

Implementation Guide

1. Peel the mango, cut the flesh, then cut it into small squares. Halve the avocado, remove the seeds, use a knife to cut into a checkered shape in the butter, then scrape the avocado core out with a spoon. Minced red onion, coriander, mixed with avocado and mango, then add olive and salt.

2. Add a little chili powder if you like it spicy, if you don't like it, just add pepper. Cut the lemon into small pieces, squeeze the juice into a bowl of avocado mango salad, mix everything and you're done. Remember to squeeze the lemon juice gently lest it become bitter.

3.Put it out on a plate and you can enjoy it. So what are you waiting for, let's try this very simple and quick salad recipe right away.

Thai Mango Salad

Element

- Ripe Mango 1 Fruit
- Bell pepper 1/2 Fruit
- Onion 1/4 Bulb
- Lemon juice 2 Tbsp

- Cucumber 1/2 Fruit

- Coriander 20 Gr

- White sugar 2 Tbsp

- Sesame Oil 1 Tbsp

- Chili powder 1 Tbsp

- Fish sauce 1 Tbsp

- Salt 1/2 teaspoon

Implementation Guide

1. Peel the mango and cut it into small pieces. Onions peeled, chopped. Bell peppers, cucumbers washed and chopped. Place all cut ingredients in a large bowl.

2.Put sugar, salt, fish sauce, lemon juice, paprika, sesame oil in a bowl, stir well so that all the spices are dissolved.

3.Coriander washed, chopped. Place the spice mixture in a bowl, mix well, then sprinkle with coriander.

4. The presentation of the dish on the plate is complete.

Fried Egg Mango Salad

Element

- Chicken Eggs 4 Eggs
- Green Mango 150 Gr
- Onion 1/2 Bulb

- Green Onion 1 Plant
- Coriander 10 Gr
- Cherry tomatoes 7 Fruits
- Fish sauce 1 Tbsp
- White Sugar 1 Tbsp
- Lemon juice 1 Tbsp
- Water 1 Tbsp
- Minced Garlic 1/2 Tbsp
- Minced chili 1/2 Tbsp
- Cooking oil 50 ml

Implementation Guide

1 Sweet and sour fish sauce includes 1 tablespoon fish sauce, 1 tablespoon sugar, 1 tablespoon lemon juice, 3 tablespoons water, 1 tablespoon minced garlic and chili, mixed in 1 cup. Cherry tomatoes cut in half, large tomatoes cut into bite-sized pieces. Green onions and cilantro cut tangled. Shredded mango. Onions cut into small pieces.

2.All put in a bowl, pour a cup of sweet and sour fish sauce and mix well.

3. Put the pan on the stove, put in 50ml of oil, wait until the oil is hot, then crack each egg into the pan and fry, evenly cooked, golden crispy on the outside, then remove to a plate lined with absorbent paper. Wait for the egg to cool, then cut the egg into bite-sized pieces (note that the cut is not too small).

4.Place eggs on a plate. Pour all the salad dressing on top and you're done. The fried egg mango salad is guaranteed to provide enough energy and still be delicious!

Tuna Salad with Kewpie Sauce

Element

- Lettuce 100 Gr
- Cherry tomatoes 4 Fruits
- Onion 1/2 Bulb
- Cucumber 1/2 Fruit

- Tuna 1/3 Box
- Roasted sesame sauce 2 Tbsp

Implementation Guide

1.Preparing ingredients for salad: Wash lettuce, cut into bite-sized pieces. Cherry tomatoes washed, cut in half. Peel the cucumber, remove the intestines and cut it into short pieces. Cut onion rings into a bowl of water with a few ice cubes available, the purpose is to reduce the pungentness and increase the crispiness of the onion.

2.Canned tuna in vinegar, take out 1/3 of the can and put it in a bowl or cup. Use a fork to crush the fish.

3.After completing the preliminary processing, take a plate for the salad on top, followed by the cucumber.

4.Next is cherry tomatoes cut in half. After another layer is the marinated tuna with vinegar.

5. Sprinkle with some sliced onion, and finally just add the Kewpie roasted sesame sauce.

6. Mix well when enjoying. Tuna salad mixed with Kewpie sauce is both quick and flavorful. Especially the fishy smell of the fish will be drowned out by this kewpie sauce.

Salmon Salad Mayo Vinegar Sauce

Element

- Green lolo lettuce 200 Gr
- Lettuce frise 100 Gr
- Cherry tomatoes 100 Gr

- Baby cucumber 100 Gr

- Purple Onion 100 Gr

- Salmon 300 Gr

- Garlic 2 Tbsp

- Parsley 2 Tbsp

- Olive Oil 4 Tbsp

- Vinegar 2 Tbsp

- White Sugar 1/2 Tbsp

- Salt 1/2 teaspoon

- Pepper 1/2 teaspoon

- Mayonnaise Sauce 30 Gr

- Yellow lemon 1/4 Fruit

Implementation Guide

1.Salmon marinated with 1/2 teaspoon salt, 1/2 teaspoon pepper, 1 tablespoon olive oil, 1 teaspoon minced garlic, 1 teaspoon minced parsley. Put everything in the salmon and then gently massage your hands, let the fish marinate for 10 minutes to absorb the spices.

2.Prepare a very hot pan, add 1 tablespoon of olive oil, add the salmon and fry for 7 minutes on each side over medium heat. Then let the fish cool down and cut it into bite-sized pieces.

3. Make the vinegar sauce: prepare 1 cup, add 1/2 teaspoon of salt, 1/2 teaspoon of pepper, 1/2 teaspoon of sugar, 2 tablespoons of vinegar, 5ml of yellow lemon juice, 1 little Grated lemon zest, 1 teaspoon minced garlic and 1 teaspoon minced parsley, mix well to combine. Finally, add 2 tablespoons of olive oil and stir well.

4. Lettuce green lot cut short. Lettuce frise cut into cubes. Cherry tomatoes cut in half. Thinly sliced baby cucumber. Purple onion cut in half then thinly sliced. Put all ingredients in a bowl, drizzle the vinegar sauce on top and mix well.

5.Pick up the salad on a plate, arrange salmon on top, spray mayonnaise on and mix well to enjoy. Your breakfast will be more nutritious when using this extremely delicious weight loss salmon salad with mayonnaise mixed with this rich source of nutrients. This salad you can eat with black bread is also very delicious! Let's save the recipe and make it right away.

Printed in Great Britain
by Amazon

38303780R00097